waterways books

Suckle

waterways.

releasing new voices, revealing new perspectives

Suckle

waterways
www.waterways-publishing.com
an imprint of flipped eye publishing

First Edition

ISBN-10: 1-905233-21-3
ISBN-13: 978-1-905233-21-2

British Library Cataloguing in Publication Data
A catalogue record for this book is available from the British Library

Editorial work for this book was supported by the Arts Council of England

Printed and Bound in the United Kingdom

For my beautiful wife Nicola Griffiths, Nicholas Makoha, Bernardine Evaristo and Peter Kahn.

Suckle

Roger Robinson
2009

Acknowledgements

I would like to thank Kevin Legendre, Grace Williams, Kwame Dawes, Nii Ayikwei Parkes, Charles Beckett and Jacob Sam-La Rose and all my family and friends who continue to support and encourage me in my work and life.

Roger Robinson

Suckle

3

4

1

Language is like milk
   — Li Young Lee

Parallel

And there under the plastic film of Gramps' album,
a picture of her in Demerara sugar sepia. 1974-short hair,
a brown dress with a thin red belt cinching waist to hips.
Her hands on curves – nearly defiant. Standing behind her

my father, grandmother and grandfather.
I was only four but I remember the clothes they wore:
It was in London and everywhere we ate Gramps
had his own pepper sauce the colour of Trinidad's dawn.

I look at the picture: the car our family car; the clothes,
the ones that would hang on the door of our small flat.
It's a mirror image of a picture in *our* album, but in ours
my mother stands right where *she* is. I look at her close –

she could pass for his sister, the spectre behind my father's
unaccountable time. The *I have to get to a meeting*,
the *I've got cricket practice*, the *I'm not made of money*,
the *I fell asleep in the car*, the sudden anger. All my life

my mother told me she dreamt my father had other children.
Repeatedly, friends have told me that they've seen my Dad's
car parked in front of a house miles away from ours,
doing weekly shopping in supermarkets in a different town.

As Gramps falls asleep, I slide the picture out and head home.
I get scissors and snip around her slim legs, carefully around
her short afro and long neck, and stick the picture on the fridge
– leaving a white space between my father and his parents.

Reading Eggs and Tea Leaves

Before baptisms in water and mourning grounds,
my mother was a practical mystic.
One who saw the future in simple little things –
like the dark green leaves from a drained morning
cup of tea or an egg broken into a glass of water.

Thin angel wings spreading in the clear water meant
that you'd have a day of luck. A billowing sail of
albumen meant you'd take a sea trip. She'd hold
the teacup at arms length and say, *Do you see? Look
at the hand, do you see the five fingers, do you see?*

And, sure enough, from the shadowed corners of the cup,
a hand would be reaching out. *It's a day for deals, son.*
But sometimes she'd read the tea leaves for a lot longer
than usual. She'd throw in a dribble of the kettle's water
swirl it around, drain it, look again and sigh and groan
and I'd ask what it was and she'd say, *Oh, it's nothing.*

Smile

(for Isele)

I cannot remember when she arrived, but I do remember when she
was there. Although she could not speak, her face always suggested
she was upset about some thing. *What's wrong?* was all I could ever
think of saying to her. She never seemed to laugh; she was always
upset with no words to explain to anyone why. And with all the
adventures of cowboy hats and toy cars, I could never understand
her sadness. Her short afro – the colour of strong tea, her round face,
and all that anger in her squinted eyes. *What's the matter?* Until one
time our father was taking a picture of us in the park. As usual she
was upset with no reason we could imagine. She tilted her cone at an
impossible angle and her ball of ice cream fell straight off in between
her shoes, the cream mound quickly melting into the green blades
of grass. This bought on a fit of adult-sized anger with flailing arms,
tears and jogging on the spot, while snot trailed from her nose. Before
my father could react, I said, *Shhh Shhh*, and gave her my ice cream.
That's the first time I remember her smiling.

Hog Plum Tree

(Pleasantville Trinidad 1976)

I was eight, at home with the maid,
Merle, when the yard-man, Keith,
came inside, already dripping.

Taking off his mud-clumped boots, he
yelled, *A storm's coming, small man!*
with a smirk, as if storms were a circus.

Hurricane Alma came so quickly,
that my parents couldn't get back
to the house from their town jobs.

Keith whispered something
to Merle who snapped her head
back laughing, then looked at me.

She walked into the bedroom
and Keith stooped down,
Small man, me and Merle

are going in that room to sleep,
so don't bother us. Just watch
TV until we wake up.

Outside the frosted window
the sky was all bruised clouds
that had turned their backs

and were scudding away.
Mosam's house of black nails,
grey wood and rusted–brown iron

sheets, blew away on the breeze,
like a metallic moth.
He ran to the next house,

but Shah's roof peeled clean off
as if lifted by God's can opener.
They all ran to Mr Beckles'.

By now the rain was coming
in sheets. It felt as though I were
looking through an angry waterfall

turning houses into ghosts.
I watched my breaths form
in haloed mists of frost.

Loose mangoes were banging
on the metal roof like gunshots.
Then came the creak and the crash

of the fallen hog plum tree and Keith
came from the room, a pale green
towel around his waist. He tied it,

slipped on his boots and walked
into the hurricane. He returned soaking,
with two buckets of golden yellow

hog plums. The ones the birds ate
before they dropped. The ones
we could never reach with stones.

The room smelled like wild honey
and Keith and I began to eat hog plums
as the rain tapped at the windows.

Haircut

My head was not right. My hair was not right.
It must have been boredom. Fourteen years old
with Dad's beard trimmer and mirror. Trimming
and trimming blindly.

Later on, walking down a packed High St. –
the only credible hangout for teenagers – I heard
the loud shriek. It was their eyes. The eyes of one
girl said *shame* and *mad*.

It spread quickly – the pointing fingers.
Did they say mangy dog? Or was it
vagrant? I can't remember. My head
was not right.

My hair was not right. I remember
trying to ignore it, it wasn't happening.
I sat on the hood of a red car.
Facing the laughing

thirty – or was it forty? I didn't want to
sit, but I couldn't move. Why was that? I should've
found a hat, but my head was not right.
So I sat. It was easier to sit.

My younger sister barged her way forward
through the crowd and stopped, her eyes
asking what was wrong with my head.
My eyes remained blank,

but her eyes said *battle* and *defend*.
She sat next to me and gave the crowd
a double–barrelled middle finger, cursing out

people's mothers. Trash

talking on their fashion sense, broad noses, bad
breath… then, as the last of them left,
bruised, she slapped my head,
Come now, let's go home.

Nest

The first Christmas without my father,
Mother calls me in to see it hanging down
over the dinner table in the living room.

Overnight a bird has squeezed through
the ventilation space and built a nest
inside the chandelier. A home inside a home.

Too pretty for a thorny crown, it is more
naïvely artistic: The natural world hugging
the light fittings' overly ornate curves.

Like mothers all over buying new curtains,
the bird has even used silver streamers
and cotton from the Christmas tree.

I imagine the homemaker spying on us
having dinner, laughing and telling stories,
watching as we prayed before we ate.

Feeling satisfied that our house felt like a home,
I picture the bird fluttering in at night, expertly
placing the first foundations of dry stalk

and then floating back to survey her work
before spying the twinkle of the Christmas
tree decorations in the starlight and thinking

Perfect. Then endless mini-flights between tree
and light, the horizon tinting the room
a marmalade pink, till the heat of the sun

fills the room and sparkles her house.
Then she sets off for her family to bring them
back to their own very homely wreath.

But the nest remained there – waiting.
As we packed our plastic tree for another year
and emptied the last of our father's clothes,

we could not bear to take down the nest.
I'm sure sometimes she flies by
to stare at the glitter – the nest she built.

The Power

We hear rattling, someone forcing the door handle.
We can hear him cursing, grunting and hitting
the door again and again – that booming sound,
shoulders on wood, his tall shadow stretching to us.

All year the news has been rife with forced entries
and gruesome slayings of whole families.
Trinidad is in the white grip of cocaine and criminals
are emboldened by guns – and numb highs.

He's probably been watching, squatting in the bushes
just outside the yard. He knows there is no father
of the house. My thirteen year old hands grasping
a carving knife, a dumbell's steel pole…

But my mother whispers, *No*, and drops to her knees
praying. She prays hard, rocking back and forth.
Prays like this was a spiritual fight, fervent and frantic.
And then the noise stops dead: nothing.

I peer out the window. No shadow, no grunting.
Opening the door slowly, I look on the patio to see a goat
with a scared look; two horns – and a gentle, gentle stare.
I take the goat by its rough horns and lead him to the road.

But the goat stands there watching, asking me questions.
I try to shoo him and he just looks at me.
I leave it there, head back inside and look
through the window just as the goat rises on its hind legs;

its horns shrink back into its head and its skin turns
from tawny grey to the dark brown of cocoa pods.
The man looks at me with those questioning eyes, gentle
eyes, before walking into the ruffling bush.

Breathing

Returning from school, you see the young black
pup lying at the side of the road. You call him
but he doesn't come, he just lies there.
You walk over and it becomes clear

that his tiny body, usually filled
with a naïve intensity, has been crushed
by a speeding car. He has used
his last reserves of energy

to get to the side of the road to die,
but he is not dead. His watery eyes
looking straight ahead, his tiny chest puffs
up and down in quick sips, as if he's run

a great distance. You lift him up
and he whimpers. His body
feels like a sack full of broken sticks.
His quick breaths press like a heartbeat

in my palms. You get an old red cushion,
place him gently in the centre of it
and take him into the garage.
You don't think he'll last the night

so you try to make him comfortable –
you put a sky-blue towel over his body
to keep him warm. The next morning
you enter the garage, expecting to have

to bury him in the hole you've dug,
but find the pup, still grabbing

quick shallow breaths of air, alive
only by the modest grace of one breath

following another. You begin to cry
at the thought of him breathing
hundreds of tiny painful breaths
with only moonlight for company.

You think that you should kill him and end it,
but when you put your hand around his tiny
neck, you can't. You think of how hard he's fought
to stay alive. So you sit in the garage,
crying, till the pup stops breathing.

Sole

Using an old dishrag to wipe away the dust,
he'd open the first Kiwi polish with a twist
and its earthy wet smell would fill the room.
He'd say that a man's shoes tell his story.

If my father saw my shoes now, my
right sole worn thin, the loose insole,
the leather scuffed, nicked and dull, the laces
frayed, he'd think that I did not take due care.

I never learned the shoe ritual: Every four
days, he'd lay two sheets of old newspaper
and line the shoes up from black to brown;
left to right, darkest to lightest.

From my football boots, he'd dig clumps of mud
with a stick and then wipe them clean with wet cloth.
His black Clarks, my black Clarks – one size
smaller, my sister's black high top Reeboks.

My mother's brown nursing shoes, my brown
church shoes, my mother's brown leather slippers.
He'd remove every lace, one hole at a time,
so that even the tongues could be cleaned.

He dipped an old toothbrush and spread the polish
like a child trying to colour between the lines.
A different polish for each shoe and shade.
A different brush for each polish.

With crumpled newspaper, a new piece
for each shoe, he'd buff and stare, buff
and stare, looking for hints of shine – then
he'd buff harder and harder still.

Each pair was then placed under our beds.
Our gleaming gifts in the half light,
stuffed with newspaper to keep proper shape.

Bubble a Pot

This is about Luther Vandross on repeat.
About a girl you loved who was no good for you.
And garlic sizzling in a blackened iron pan
with cubes of beef huddled like bricks
on onion circles. And ground green seasoning paste.

This is about men and stories of women
that they should and should not have broken up
with – others they stayed with far too long –
and about women they loved and left on a whim.
Women are crazy, says Markie, and they all nod.

This is about men with too-full mouths, mumbling
agreement when I ask if I've done the right thing,
while passing the sliced tomato salad with salt;
myriad stories of love being told and retold
as they tell me now that they never liked her.

This is about men smothering food with pepper sauce,
making lime juice with brown sugar – from scratch –
belching without apology, while eating spoonfuls of rice.
This is about men enacting rituals without knives
and forks, eating till the food is *done*.

This is about men who journeyed from their homes
with food – a five pound bag of basmati rice, four green limes,
three pounds of cubed beef, golden vegetable oil,
four garlic cloves and fresh market tomatoes –
because they know all about break-ups and closed curtains.

The Cures

My mother's got prayers.
Prayers for hot food and smiling visitors.
Prayers for aunts who see ghosts
in their houses after divorce. My mother's
got prayers for wiry youth
and scowling generations. Each one
a ritual of release rising
all the way to heaven like prayer
candles' curling smoke.
My mother's got prayers for cousins
in cults, prayers for families whose fathers
moved in with other women.
My mother's got prayers for diabetics,
for the creeping blue ice of cancer,
for stiff arthritic claws, for the droop
of the impotent and the blood of the infertile.
My mother's got prayers tucked in old books,
in new bibles, under fridge magnets,
in kitchen cupboards, on CD
and DVD… See, you've got to shut
your eyes real real tight
to make a request to God. To talk to him
like that – the belief in her voice.
It made me wonder about God and her;
if there was a small, powerful God
glowing like lit coal inside her chest
that burned hot with each verse.
My mother's got prayers for flights,
for sons in cold countries at Christmas.
Prayers to cover her family and friends
– like a gossamer web of God's spirit.
Each declaration, a dying breath;
each pause for breath, a life everlasting.

Kite

It was my first act of will and therefore my first act of memory, I must have been three – definitely not four. As my father filled up on gas, the Esso station gave him a free promotional kite, which he handed to me. A white kite with a blue and red logo in the centre. I decided that day I would fly it. As we drove back home, a snowstorm began to set in over Edinburgh. Already my parents were trying to convince me that perhaps the weather conditions weren't right. I said nothing – I would fly. We got home and the snow was coming down in sheets. But before my father could say no, I was already pulling on my boots. With my coat on and kite in my hand, I ran in the snow, up and down, but the kite would not lift off. My father came out and said, *It won't work son, the snow is too much.* I remember saying I nearly had it. It flew a little bit. He stood in the doorway watching me until somehow I decided to jump off the short wall at the front. I felt a tug on the line and ran and ran and it was up – flying. Looking at my parents watching from the doorway, shaking their heads, I said, *look, you see,* and watched my kite dodge the snowflakes.

Emperors

In Trinidad I didn't dare spray walls –
too many people watching
and we didn't have any trains to paint on.
When the beat kicked in, from the boom box
or the boom-bap of palms and fists on desks,
I was never the dancer; far too fat

for windmills, far too clumsy
for backspins. I was the guy at the side
of the circle keeping up the vibe.
I was the guy with a soul clap and a big smile.
My local crew was called *The Emperors*.
Pleasantville, San Fernando, Trinidad's greatest.

And I was its only non breaking member.
I did the practical things, the support:
Someone had to carry the linoleum.
Someone had to adjust the equaliser.
And when our only videotape of Graffiti Rock
popped, it was I who lovingly untangled

the ribbon from the VCR head.
It was I who stole my mother's
bronze nail varnish and spliced the tape
back together with barely a stutter on the screen.
I even made war notes on the best crews
and discussed counter-move choreography.

And when we burned crews, we jumped and hugged.
And when a boy tried to slap me because they lost,
right on the blood-red tiles in the centre of the mall,
my crew beat him down. And his crew
just stood aside and watched, as we chanted;
Emperors Emperors Emperors Emperors.

The Stand Pipe

Right there, on the corner, was where
you'd fill your iron bucket if you had no water.

Every morning on my way to school
I'd see people waiting for their chance.

In my starched white shirt and pleated
pants I waited for a taxi, looking at them.

Their lives seemed so simple. Days started
with getting two buckets of clean water.

Wives would gossip until it was their turn.
Kids would walk uphill in measured steps

with a filled bucket half their size.
Sometimes grown men would strip off,

down to their underpants, and lather up
right there – blue soap and frothy beards.

Naked tots were baptised in public,
mothers shampooing shapes in their hair.

Gallons of water flowed as women washed
their families' clothes, their fists riding

the ridges of the scrubbing board, making clothes
white again with the chlorine smell of bleach.

Now a mother is walking away with a full bucket

for her coffee, a naked baby perched on her hip.

And a man with grey hair pulls white pockets
out of his khakis and sees me looking at him.

The End of the Bread Van

The babble of our feel-bad laughter in the shade of the samaan tree.
Our powerlessness on display for all the older generations with work.
Twice a day the bread van would pull up with beef pies, soft drinks
                                                and cakes.

We the young men of Blitz Village had nowhere to go in the mornings.
It was 1982, when Texaco sucked all Trinidad's oil and ran away with
                                                the money.
The babble of our feel-bad laughter in the shade of the samaan tree.

So we headed to the bench on the corner, bright and early, as if
                                                it were work.
We'd sit there telling stories, laughing and shouting, a noisy unemployed
                                                chorus.
Twice a day the bread van would pull up with beef pies, soft drinks
                                                and cakes.

Food so cheap and filling that even we could afford it with coins
                                                from our pockets.
The bread van broke up the boredom floating the day past our
                                                blank eyes.
So we headed to the bench on the corner, bright and early, as if
                                                it were work.

Singh, who drove the bread van, was barely older than we were.
He sometimes even gave us a three-pie credit because he knew
                                                our plight.
Food so cheap and filling that even we could afford it with coins
                                                from our pockets.

But that did not stop young Andre, who'd sit with us eating beef pies
each day,
from sneaking up alongside Singh's bread van – right when we were
buying food.
Singh, who drove the bread van, was barely older than we were.

With his mother's stocking over his head and a gun in one hand,
he sneaked up to Singh –
wearing the same white shirt and khaki shorts he'd wear every day.
Stick up!
Young Andre who'd sit with us eating beef pies each day.

He shouted and pointed the gun into the window. The van sped off,
and Singh yelled back, *You think I don't know it's you Andre?!*
With his mother's stocking over his head and a gun in one hand.

Recall

The jump, the shout, the running at break. And the grass, so much grass. The way it scratched our skins when we fell. The friends sitting in the crook of a twisted tree branch trying to cool the sweat. The breeze like meditation. The way we sat without talking. The year I fell in love only with girls whose name began with W. The songs we sang to broken mornings. The year I challenged everyone I knew, and every one I met, to a race. The wind on my face, the victories. The stones we threw at the red blush of ripe mangoes. The green cherries we shook. Their dry tart taste edging our teeth. The hand I burned trying to steal hot fudge. The other hand I burned trying again. The six-million-dollar man lunch kit that I laid into a bully's head. The six-million-dollar man flask that shattered. The way it sounded like a jar of stars when it shook. The pirate costume my mother made for the school carnival. The eye patch, the head-tie scarf. How I jumped to the music. How proud I was as I danced. The butterflies I chased before Common Entrance exams. The angry teacher. The way he pushed me down the row of hunched boys at desks. The empty seat. The dog having its puppies on the couch. The way she'd only let me hold them. The way she'd snap at any- one else. How many yellow sun yolks did I burst? How much of my sister's food did I eat? The holiday in Disneyland where I wore tennis shorts. The hours my sister and I queued singing the chorus of 'Sweet Dreams Are Made Of This' like a chant. The Christmas dinners of flat pastelles, potato salad mountains, and deep seas of red sorrel. The trips to the beach where Mum would make us sit on the sand for two hours after eating. The sea daring us with every breaking wave. The salt, the sea on our tongues.

2

Griffiths

Grififths's dad marched up the college hill.
A man with an angry walk, a man with a stick.
He grabbed Griffiths – the school thug – by his shirt,
pulling him to the centre of the football field,
their dark brown skins clear against the sandy field.

His father raised his switch and we heard
the swoosh and the thwack of each stroke.
It looked like a man beating a small replica
of himself. The backswing of each lash so high
it seemed to be pointing at the relentless sky.

Griffiths stood upright with his hands
on his head. Soon the teachers stopped teaching
and student heads crowded the windows.
He was a hated boy in the halls of school.
He robbed the younger and weaker of money.

But nobody wanted this. After the fifteenth stroke
some boys and teachers were in tears, still watching
this very public execution. By the twentieth stroke
we noticed our principal's paunch bobbing
quickly towards the scene and physically stopping

the beating. The father threw down the cane,
turned and started walking without looking back.
Griffiths collapsed into the principal's hug.
O forgive the bleaching sun, O forgive the father.
O forgive the witnesses, O Griffiths, Griffiths.

More

The smell of molasses from Vat 19 Distillers
as I drive past on the Beetham Highway,

overwhelms me, rekindles my feelings of home.
It's all iron and ash and flaming cane syrup.

It's the smell of my mother throwing brown sugar
into hot oil as it bubbles to a rich brown caramel.

It's the smell of Christmas cake, rich with fruit
soaked in rum since last Christmas.

It's the punch-a-crème filled with condensed milk
and rum so thick you wait for it to pour itself.

The stale breath of cigarettes, rum and coke on uncles
who stab themselves with needles dripping insulin.

It's the aftertaste of rum that gave my grandmother
a stroke, that made her lose the use of her legs.

She asks me to massage them for her, and I rub
her stiff thighs with Ben-Gay, its eucalyptus smell

burning my nose as she tells me about the first time
she had a drink – she was just eleven. She said

the rum made her feel so good that she would save
all her money just so she could drink rum every day.

I think of all the roads she walked

between fields with tall green stalks of cane

that stretched to the sky; of all the fly-ridden
donkey carts of cane heading for the distillers.

Now here is that smell again, that molasses smell
– the sweetness and sorrow.

The Bringing Back

Bert does not understand why the vet wants to kill his dog. How can he understand dog years? The dog at ten, the same age as him. He struggles with the dead weight of the Alsatian. *Come on we're going home, no one's killing my dog.*

But Bert understands care. At home he cuts four holes in an old white bed sheet for each of the dog's feet. Tying a harness to a garage beam with a box and a pillow for the dog's slouched neck.

Every day I watch him put cooked chicken in the blender and take it to the dog's mouth with a spoon and tell him to *Eat, come on eat!* finally taking the pap in his hands, opening the dog's jaws and placing the food onto the tongue.

He starts to sleep on a spare mattress in the garage; staring at the drowsy eyes of his dog. He bends each leg one hundred times twice a day, strokes his tan and black fur, and prays for his dog to live. Five days later I smile as I hear a bark and see the dog running around the garden. And Bert opens the door shouting, *He's back, he's back!*

Shelling the Peas

We sit around a dark green hill
of peas, so high it looks impossible
to flatten; all of us – mothers, aunties
girl cousins, and me – twisting open
the tiny coffins of pods
to expose perfect green pearls.
Running a finger along a cracked seam,
Aunty Ann speaks about how Mama
used to be able to make any dress
from any catalogue; you'd wake up
and the replica dress would be there.
My mother says that she thinks Mama
was ready to die and wanted to see
her family in England one last time.
Some shells reveal worms wriggling,
some peas are light brown and rotting –
my mother eats the fresh green ones
raw. She remembers how Mama
liked to bet on the horses and the lottery
right to the very end. A spider scampers
from the small hill of peas, zigzagging
in the direction of Aunty Lynette. She jumps
up on her chair and they all laugh
until they start to cry.

Patrick

And what of you, Patrick McIntyre:
who kept a growing wasp's nest
in your desk the entire first form
without getting a single sting.

You who emerged from the forest
behind our school with a snake
round your neck, *making everyone
scatter away as you walked past.*

You who never once gave an answer,
connected to any question the teacher
ever asked, but continually put up
your hand as if you were the class swot.

Your blonde unwashed hair growing
past your shoulder, you were constantly tucking
your shirt in your pants. Your tab
at the sno-cone lady was over fifty dollars.

I could not think of how you could pass
any exams with all of those thoughts
of insects and reptiles. I tried to speak
to you but you spoke a syntax of tangents.

People said that you'd seen your father
having sex with an '*outside*' woman
and that it tripped a fuse in your brain.

Others said that you were not mad at all.

Some people said that you were a genius,
on some plane that we as mere schoolboys
could never understand. Others said
that your chest held the heart of a lizard.

Patrick, I'm married now. Did you ever
find a mate? Someone who understood
all your animal thoughts. Or do the bees
still buzz and crawl through your brain?

Mr. Lee Wah moves Mountains

San Fernando Hill was being slowly scraped
away to gravel by yellow bulldozer claws.

Vice Principal, Lee Wah, planned a protest;
all people had to do was grab a placard.

Mr Lee Wah wrote the Bristol board signs: *Don't
Kill Our Hill* – stapled to broomsticks.

On the day, there was only him and the signs.
He waited and waited and nobody else came.

Finally in the centre of La Romain roundabout
he grabbed all ten placards and stood in the hot sun.

A one-man protest as cars zoomed past and beeped.
People pointed and laughed. The newspapers came.

The headlines on the next day told of a madman's
protest. Jokes were made about him at lunch breaks.

There were calls to stop him from teaching.
That school year he barely left his office;

he just sat at his desk, with a thousand yard stare,
his spirit ground down to rock and rubble.

Miss Jagroop

The heavy curve of your breasts grazed our shoulders
as you checked over our comprehension homework.
You'd pull some pouting pose every five minutes
with your butter fat rear spreading all over our desks.
Did you smell our musky adolescent scent?
Did you breathe us all in? All our stale breaths?
We liked you as much as we were embarrassed.
The charged atmosphere made us drunk with desire.
But when you ran your hands through Gerard's hair
and told him that he was becoming so handsome,
that all the young ladies must be queuing up for him.
When you held his gaze and bit your bottom lip
for three or four silent seconds, the only thing we could do
was look at our muddy shoes like the boys we were.

Sergeant

His skin was a deeper shade of dark
through dirt or sun – I still can't tell.
Only the greasiness of his skin helped
to tell flesh from torn black clothes.

He never begged. He simply lay
outside Royal Castle Fried Chicken.
And folks would give him a portion
of chips or leftover biscuits and coleslaw.

It's said that he was a soldier in the US Army,
that he was the director of the music corps.
But he fell in love with this Yankee woman
who stole his mind and never gave it back.

So they sent him back with wild darting eyes
and grey bin bags filled with his belongings.
Sometimes he'd pull out a golden coronet
and blow tunes so melancholic, even

the angry, hustling taxi drivers hummed.

The Blade's Edge

Boy I end up getting in ah set of confusion
when you was away. It wasn't good.
Things was real, real rough and I end up chopping a man
with a cutlass. Don't look at me that way – he not dead.
Jus lissen to dis and tell me what you woulda do.

Well you know Mums does go away and make she hustle
in Venezuela, but usually she gone for two weeks
and come back with cash, food, and some clothes.
Well, boy, this time – two weeks gone, one month gone, two months
gone; and all we food and money done after the first month.

So I'm there and my sista ain't have no shoes for school
and my two next brothas telling me they hungry.
The worse part is that she leave my next sista who is one.
The baby crying for milk and losing plenty weight.
So I end up leaving she by the brown-skin lady next door.

And I know the brown-skin lady is a nice lady, but still
the baby can't stay there long cause she have no money either.
And, boy, I looking for work everywhere but they see
a ghetto youth like me and is 'no' every time.
So I had to do something. Get things in hand.

Then a policeman offer me twenty thousand dollars
to chop a man. Well, that was plenty money for me.
My brothas and sistas could live for a year on that.
And I'm not hearing a word from Mums at all.
No work, no money, so I end up chopping a man.

Uncle Karl and the Summer Girl

That summer, Karl returned to Trinidad with a girl.
She was red haired with a neck like an alabaster vase
and skin that goes blotchy in the sun but never tans.

She seemed happy but never said much.
She kept her questions and answers to a few words.
Most of the time she'd read books on the patio.

They would go out most evenings and she'd return,
smiling, with the coppery scent of rum in her wake.
She'd drift off into sleep at the table mid-meal.

One evening Karl tells me that she's his whore,
she's here to make him money while he stays
and that men would give two months wages for her.

Each day I'd see the eyes of bare-backed men,
slowing down to catch a glimpse of her
sunning herself in shades and floral bikini tops.

Each evening she'd return looking more unhappy.
Each day she read less, sitting hypnotised by the TV.
Karl would give her a look and then they'd leave.

I woke up one morning to see Karl eating alone.
He told me that the summer girl had gone back.
The work here was just too hard for her.

3

Electric Boogaloo

In 1984 my sister was serious about dancing.
She was the only girl dancer in the Emperor's
dance crew. Probably the only girl breaker
in Trinidad, but that wasn't enough for her.
She never entered the centre of a battle
because she thought she was not good enough.
She wanted to be better than the boys.
Straight from school she'd go
to her bedroom slam the door and you'd hear
the click of her boom box followed by the synths
of *Rock rock the planet rock, don't stop.*
She could pick up dances as if by osmosis.
It would take me weeks of practice for simple steps
but she only needed thirty seconds of intense looking
and she'd have it – and then a minute to better it.
So when the New York City breakers, the world's best
breaking crew came to Trinidad, my sister was front row
staring the whole two hours at Mr Wiggles – the king
of electric boogaloo. Uprock specialist. As he bent
twisted like molten plastic, limbs like rubber,
I knew something serious was happening.
As soon as we got home she headed to her room
and slammed the door. There was the click of the tape
and I heard hand claps of *Clap your hands everybody
cause you got what it takes.* At the next dance battle,
her allegiance hidden under her blouse, she stood
watching. As the battle heated up, my sister removed
layers to reveal her *Emperor* shirt and jumped in
to commence battle, her whole body becoming fluid.
A girl with superior uprock skills – better than any boy.
Emperors win again. *Emperors Emperors Emperors.*

The Flying Man's Lament

As soon as shackles were taken off the first slaves, they all just floated up and flew from the deck, back to their own lands. Leaving slavers red-faced and open-mouthed. That's when the crew, fearful for their own lives, decided to keep their flying bounty chained in the ship's belly. And after the first meal of salted fish the crew saw the slaves lose fight. They could barely stand much less fly.

I still fly because I was breast-fed all the way – salt free. Even here I only eat ripe fruit from the tops of trees. When I was younger I used to think about flying away. You know, my wife and I would argue and I would just take off into the air – but then my wife would hold our baby up, and I'd just float back down to the dirt in the yard.

None of my children can fly. Salt lovers – all of them. They take after their mother. My granddaughter dreams of floating over mountains; her mother insists on feeding her fried chicken, pizzas – all sorts of nonsense. Like her my feet are stuck on the ground, but I am thinking of sky.

Limes

Uncle Clyde is refusing to buy coke.
He says we've limes at home in the yard.
The picking of, the slicing, the squeezing –
some with juice, others with nothing but seed.

He empties half a bag of brown sugar
and mixes, but the granules refuse to melt.
A tray of ice cubes from the fridge freezer
dips and floats as water fills the jug.

After the grit of sugar on our tongues,
after the gulps and ahhs, Uncle Clyde laughs.
Now tell me, isn't that better than coke?
And he doesn't even wait for an answer.

Mama

You used to love your coffee.
The inside of all your mugs stained
a muddy brown. Never instant,
but neither did you have a coffee machine.

It was a simple coffee, sieve and cup situation.
The steaming water gliding past the granules
oh so slowly. One strong coffee could take
up to fifteen minutes to brew to the strength

you said could make you feel alive again.
You'd toss the bitter smelling dregs,
the caffeinated swill would settle in the grass
and start seeping into the mud.

It's been many years now since
you've been buried, but every time it rains
I think of the coffee pulp
filtering through the earth.

Rich coffee falling to your mouth
the burnt taste licked off your bottom lip,
your eyes flickering open for a minute

saying, *Ahh! now that feels a lot better.*

The Urgency of Sound

1.
Uncle Clyde had acquired a collection
of old calypsonians on shellac 45s.
Each started with a prolonged scratch
and hiss. As the orchestras kicked in
and the singing hit, you could see him
doing the silliest of made up dances.
Not for my entertainment; that
was what the music made him do.
It bent him down, it straightened him up.
It made him roll his shoulders.
It twisted and tangled him till he forgot
that I was even there.

2.
Trinidad, Carnival 2005.
I'm settling back in and I'm walking
the streets. Then from nowhere
I hear a song and all I can do is dance.
I'm taking off my shirt
and waving it over my head.
And everything I can feel has now moved
up past my neck into my head.
It's too much, so I have to close
my eyes. By the second chorus,
I know the words, and the words know me.
I'm singing along. *If your clothes
tear up and your shoes mash up,
you could still jump up when music
playing.* I hear the song
ten minutes later – and it happens again.

The Misuse of Magic

Your grandfather always had a way of just showing up. You would never hear him, and suddenly he'd be right behind you. Breathing. The burnt sugar smell of rum on his breath. Paydays were worse. I had a code for the children to get to their rooms and not come out. I'd sing the hymn 'A Little More Oil in My Lamp' and the kids would scurry into the bedroom – all ten of them.

He'd lose his money gambling and drinking, and he'd come home angry, start an argument and eventually punch me. When it was in the face I really couldn't take it. Going to the market to buy food and everybody watching, looking at the swelling. It was the shame, not the pain, that made me decide to get out.

One time he turned up, sat down outside on the patio and shouted that he wanted a chicken sandwich. I jumped. I didn't even know he was outside. He knew we didn't have no chicken. I told the children to make him a sandwich with the spinach in the fridge. He just ran inside shouting I ask for you to make it not her and he threw me on the ground against the wall. As he was coming toward me I braced myself against the wall and kicked him in the chest as hard as I could and he passed out drunk.

*

Coins disappear through only two things; a hand and a coin

*

The children need money for new shoes for school.

*

Papa papa stop, you'll kill her.

*

A little more oil in my lamp keeps it burning

A little more oil in my lamp I pray

*

"nor… can I leave you a strong garrison: but I shall give you strength."

*

with style, with grace…

*

No new curtains for Christmas again.

*

But look at my crosses.

*

If I never learned to sew then my children wouldn't have no clothes.

*

We're playing that game again: under the bed, hands on ears and see if you could hear your heart and count your breaths till you reach to 100.

*

Love as strong as death itself.

*

Central to all of this was the story of gender.

*

The magician destroys an object and restores it.

*

Even when I got on the bus after I'd been hiding at a friend's house for two weeks: as the bus pulled off I peeped outside the window over the seat – there he was getting smaller in the distance. Even when I got on the ship and was pulling into the port in London, I saw some-one that looked like him and I had to stare just to make sure.

Gramps

In the dream there was a knocking at our door
I opened it and you were in your vest
with blue chequered shorts, and no shoes.

You say, *They've stolen all my furniture!* and I
say, *Don't worry gramps I have money
I'll replace them. That's not the point!* you say.

*You young people today do not know the value
of money. We have to build it all from scratch,
and you have to help me. Gramps I'm very busy*

with my work, I don't have time. Then we are
in your empty house looking at pictures of your lost
possessions. You start sawing, and you're becoming

younger with each piece of wood cut, till we're the same
age, and you no longer need your glasses. You rest
your walking stick and your stiff leg bends easily.

When we get to building your work desk, you tell me
that when the desk is finished you will die. So I say,
Let us not build the desk. But you say, *We must.*

So we saw, looking at each other while we work.
We measure and saw some more, until I look up
and you're not there –

just an empty room with new furniture.

Snowdome

Parting the dense brush of her hair
into equidistant parts, exposing

a thin track of skull. Combing both
sides apart, willing them to stay down.

My mother's head slightly bowed
like some shamed child. She is seated

on the ground, in the v of my father's
legs, as he sits on the edge of the couch

overlooking her head, the flakes of dandruff
in the gap like a road of strewn stones.

He places the point of the comb in the parting
and traces the line back and forth.

My father, the farmer, plows her head
and they gossip about their friends,

the flakes of dandruff floating slowly down,
surrounding my mother like a snowdome.

Visiting Uncle Francis

Pregnant pods of cocoa hang from trees.
The door of his wooden hut swings open.
He edges out on the balls of his feet
with a stick raised high, poised to strike,
as crickets play percussion into the night.

Uncle Francis, I say, *It is me.*
He adjusts his grip and stares. *Who are you
and how do you know me?*
His accent has a Spanish lilt to it.
I'm Florence's grandson, I've come to see you.

He blinks his hazel eyes and slowly lowers
his weapon, transforming it to walking aid.
Head inclined to the ground, he looks up,
shakes my hand, carefully searching my face.
His palms are raw leather. *Come let's drink.*

Inside his hut is a study – clean and basic,
a canvas hammock, a glowing kerosene lamp,
two upturned iron buckets with cushions.
See how the rum turned my hair white like clouds?
Skin glowing bronze in the lamplight,

he pours me a clear glass.
He raises his and says, *To family.*
To family, I say, and drink, cough and sputter.
He pats me on the back and says,

I see that you're not a thirsty man.

He continues drinking and smiling;
telling me about the time some men
in the village plotted to kill him
because he'd slept with their wives
and daughters, about how his stick

has stopped sharpened cutlasses.
He tells me that in thirty stickfight battles,
he split ten men's heads, but killed only one;
shows me the dark stains on the stick
and talks about hard estate work.

He stokes his kerosene lamp and I
tell him of my wife, writing and my new house.
Handing me a bottle of coconut water,
he says, *If you're lucky maybe one day
family may just come to look for you too.*

4

Rum Shop

These men drink white rum like soda,
smiles lingering long on their lips.
Whenever there's a need for them to be
found, their children – in faded clothes
and threadbare rubber slippers – walk down
the street to deliver urgent messages of need
from their wives, girlfriends or lovers
and they react with a drunkard's outrage.
They watch young girls walking home
from school and talk about how many women
they've had. One talks about he likes
his women young – before their breasts turn
from rubber to sponge – and boasts about
sometimes having to sex a mother
to get to her fourteen-year-old daughter.
The rum prevents any shame that's cast
from reflected children in the bottle's curve.
They feel a glow of heat to the chest.
They have small beads of rum sweat on their forehead.
They are a sweet forgetting, and a zigzagged
route to their house with one eye open.
They are a waking and wanting not to.
They are a slow walk back like a funeral
to the rum shop to share a riddle
that they will never be able to work out.

What the Midnite Robber Said

No my friend don't smile with me. I'll pull those gleaming white teeth and roll them like dice on the pavement. I'll leave you with just purple fleshy gums and the metallic taste of your own blood, gathering and flooding your mouth.

Stop your suffering now, I beg of you! You think I like leaving all them bones and dripping flesh in the Beetham dump? You think I enjoyed that? No sir I did not. Stop now. Give me the money I need to be on my way.

And what about your family? Don't you think they'll be sad? I have to let you know that I feel it better to slay them than let them live with the weight of your gruesome death pressing, pressing down on them. So pay me, for their sake.

You think what I do is easy? I assure you it is not. I wish I could feel the fear that you feel right now.

Pleasantville Hibiscus

You're beauty in hair,
respect in a young man's suit.
You are thick-veined hands
in an old widow's garden.
You're a grave's final goodbye.

Two Miracles of the Feast

1.
He told the show-off American girl
to take out those big silver-hoop earrings.
Warned her a spirit could just fly through
them and get her, but she paid him no mind,
said she didn't believe that mumbo jumbo.
The drums rolled and the chant caught rhythm
and she found herself being pulled to her knees.
Her head became pinned to the ground,
right cheek anchored down in the dust.
She screamed for help and they all watched,
knowing that they couldn't cross the will
of the spirits. He was the one who walked over
and unhooked the first and then the second silver circle
from her head and helped the dusty, crying girl up.

2.
Merle knew that she hadn't finished cooking
the food for the offerings. She wanted to join in.
She heard booming bass from the speakers,
so she turned off the blue-flamed stove,
took a shower, put on her make up and rose perfume
and walked down the hill to the pulsing music.
As soon as she met her friends, she was thrown
to the floor, and the spirits began to roll her through
all the revellers. Chunky trainers and slim high heels
stepped quickly away to avoid being mown over.
Ogun and Legba rolled her, gathering speed up the hill
to her house. She opened the door, went straight
to the kitchen, turned the blue flame back on
and began to peel the carrots – without changing clothes.

The New La Diablesse

for the sex tourists of Tobago

I wear my long white cotton skirt
so no man will see my cow foot.

I can smell the death on each man who looks
at me with that lustful eye. It's a scent

much like the smell of mould, semen
and wet earth. That smell is what I live for.

The ones who can control their nature
can see me for what I really am:

The faithful, the very old, the very young,
some of the clergy and the strictly gay,

they can hear the clicking of my hoof,
see the hop and drop nature of my walk.

To those young men seeking experience,
husbands cheating on their wives. The vain,

the opportunists, the experimenters, the kinky –
I am the bait for hell, the ecstatic funk of death.

Perverted doom, freaky eternal suffering heat.
I'm the La Diablesse. Burn, burn with my love.

Rum, Sugar and the Lash

The cane, the cutlass, the sugar.
The translucent reflection in the bottles
 from cane cut by Indian men in the fields

sitting cross-legged eating their roti
at lunchtime, listening to the cricket
on a light-green transistor radio hissing static.

They open a small flask of white rum
to make the day go faster; the smell
of burnt sugar, the gurgle, the heat

like a delta growing through their chests.
The press, the juice, the boiler.
The grating sound the wooden spoon

makes against the sugar and cloves
in the yellow bucket of red sorrel drink
that we'll sip throughout Christmas.

The snap, the crack of the rum bottle's seal,
the clinking of the ice, the tributary swig
poured out for the spirits of those long gone.

The bite, the blood, the flesh.
The slaves that ran away and got caught,
then ran away again to get caught by dogs.

The whipping, the screams, the criss-crossed,
raised keloid scars like a tangle of snakes.

The rope, the noose, the burning.

The black ash drifting down for days and days
from the smouldering cane fields, burnt to chase snakes
away, before being cut by Indian men in straw hats.

We Hope You Enjoyed Reading!

Let us know what you think by sending an e-mail to
editor@waterways-publishing.com

Thank You for buying *Suckle*. If you would like more information about waterways publishing, please join our mailing list online at **www.waterways-publishing.com**.

Visit our other imprints online:

mouthmark *(poetry)*
www.flippedeye.net/mouthmark

lubin & kleyner *(fiction)*
www.flippedeye.net/lubinandkleyner

flipped eye *(general)*
www.flippedeye.net